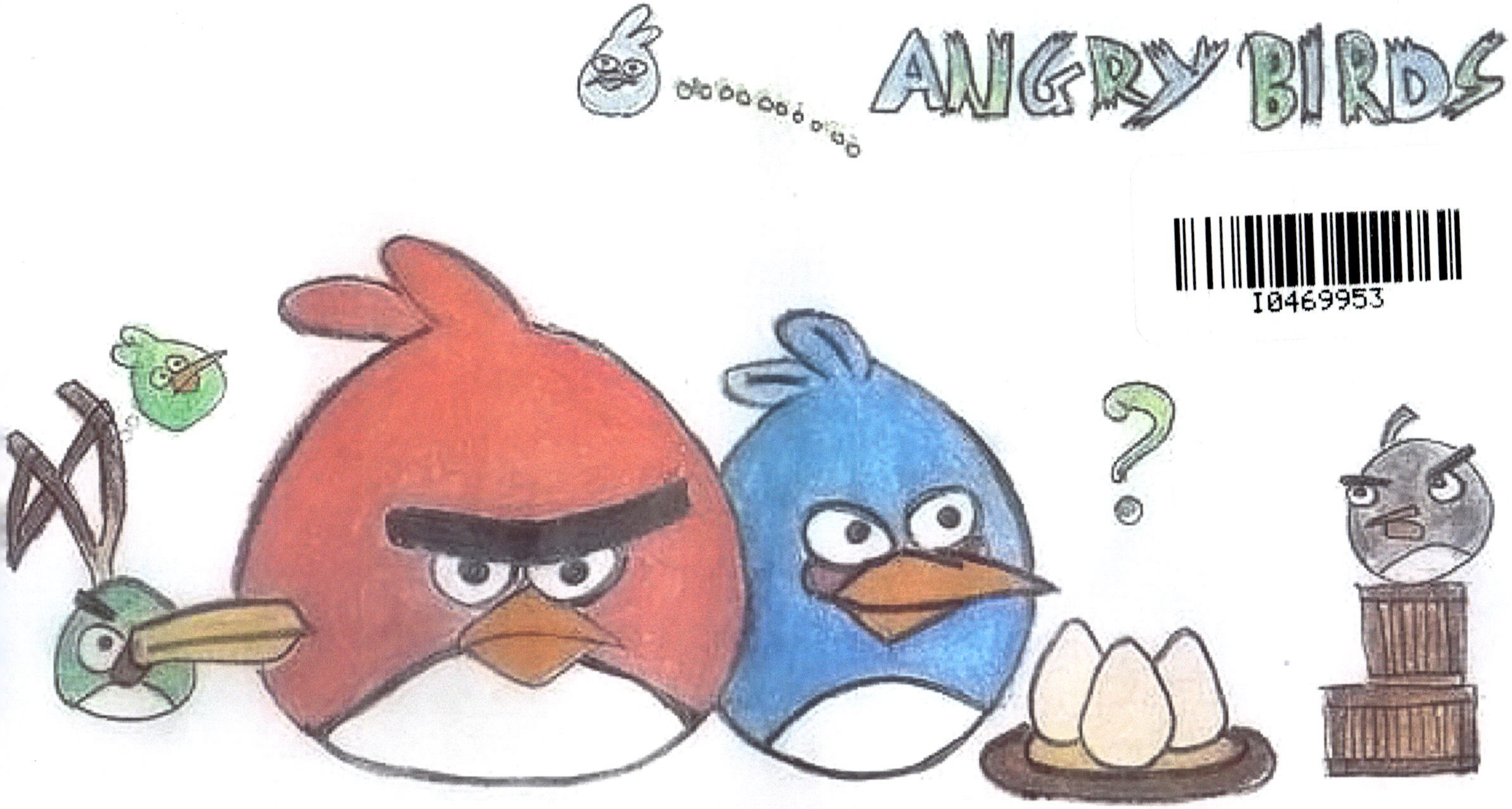

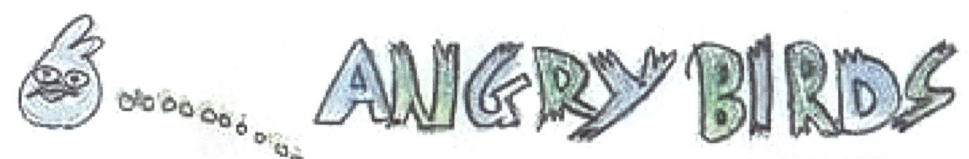

How to Draw Cartoons

By: Sourabh Aryabhatta

First Printing: October 2015

For information on services offered by Sourabh Aryabhatta, visit the following link.

https://www.guru.com/freelancers/sourabh-aryabhatta

ISBN-13: 978-1518763366
ISBN-10: 1518763367

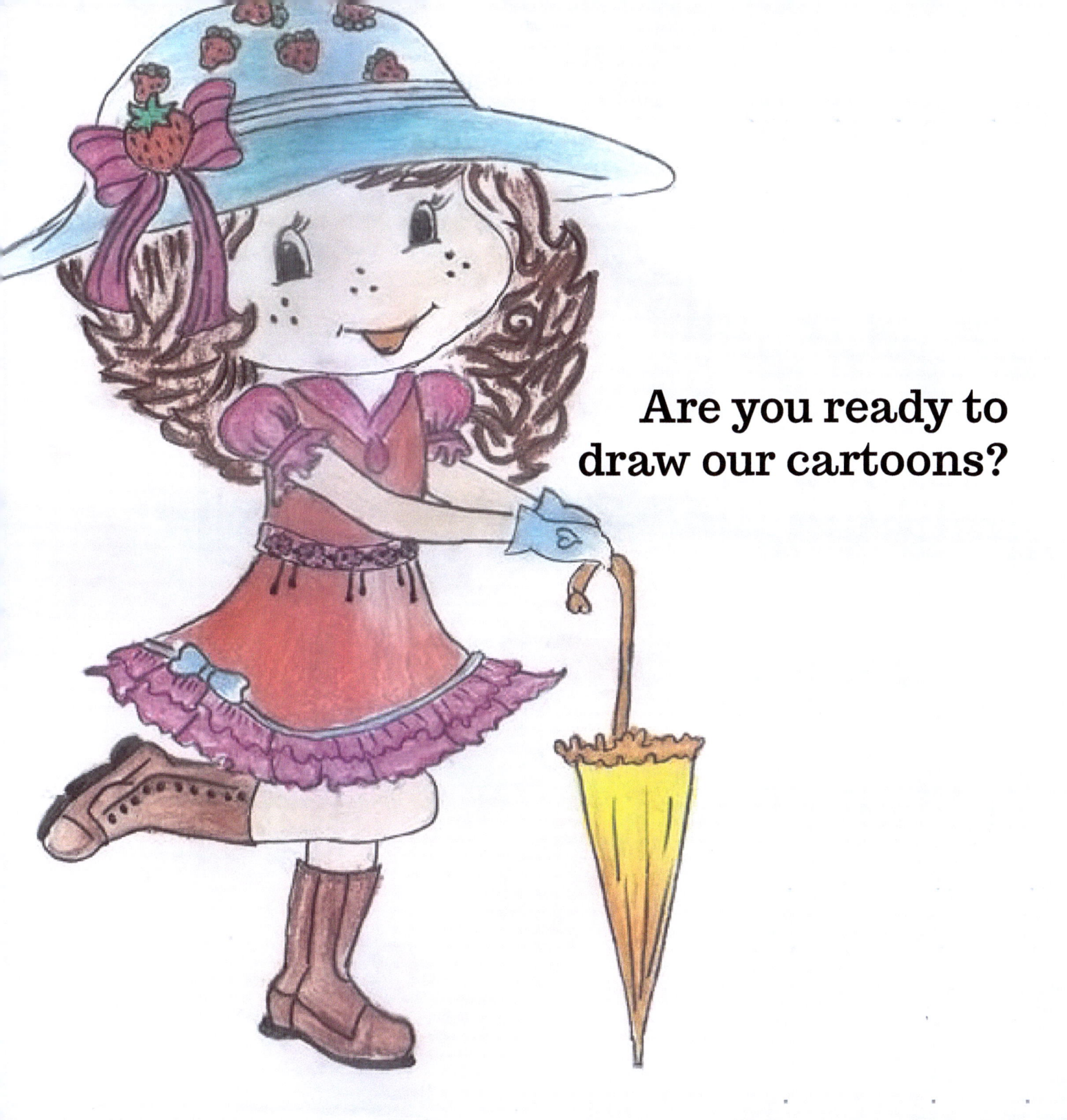

Are you ready to draw our cartoons?

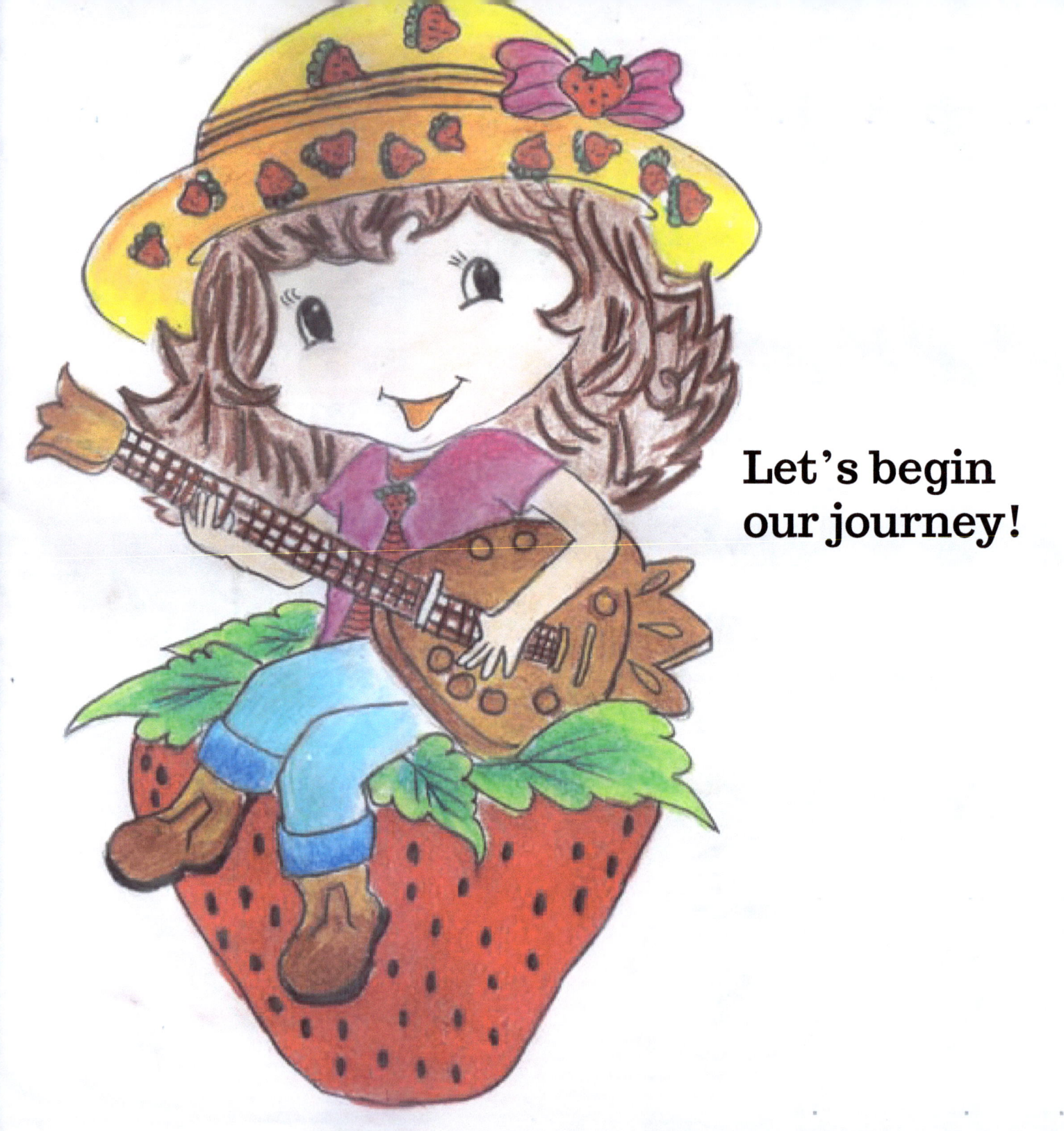

Let's begin
our journey!

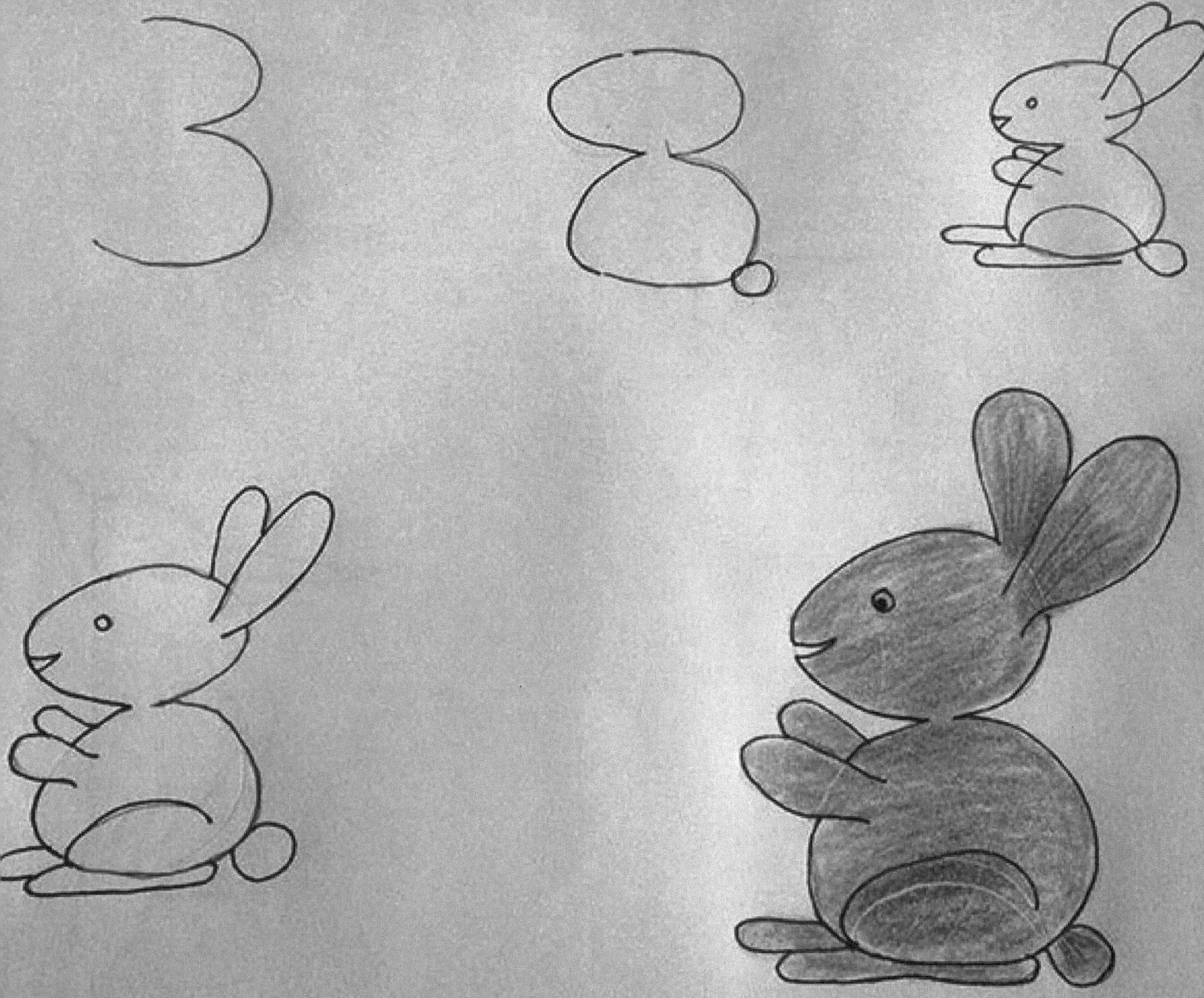

Wow, it's a rabbit!

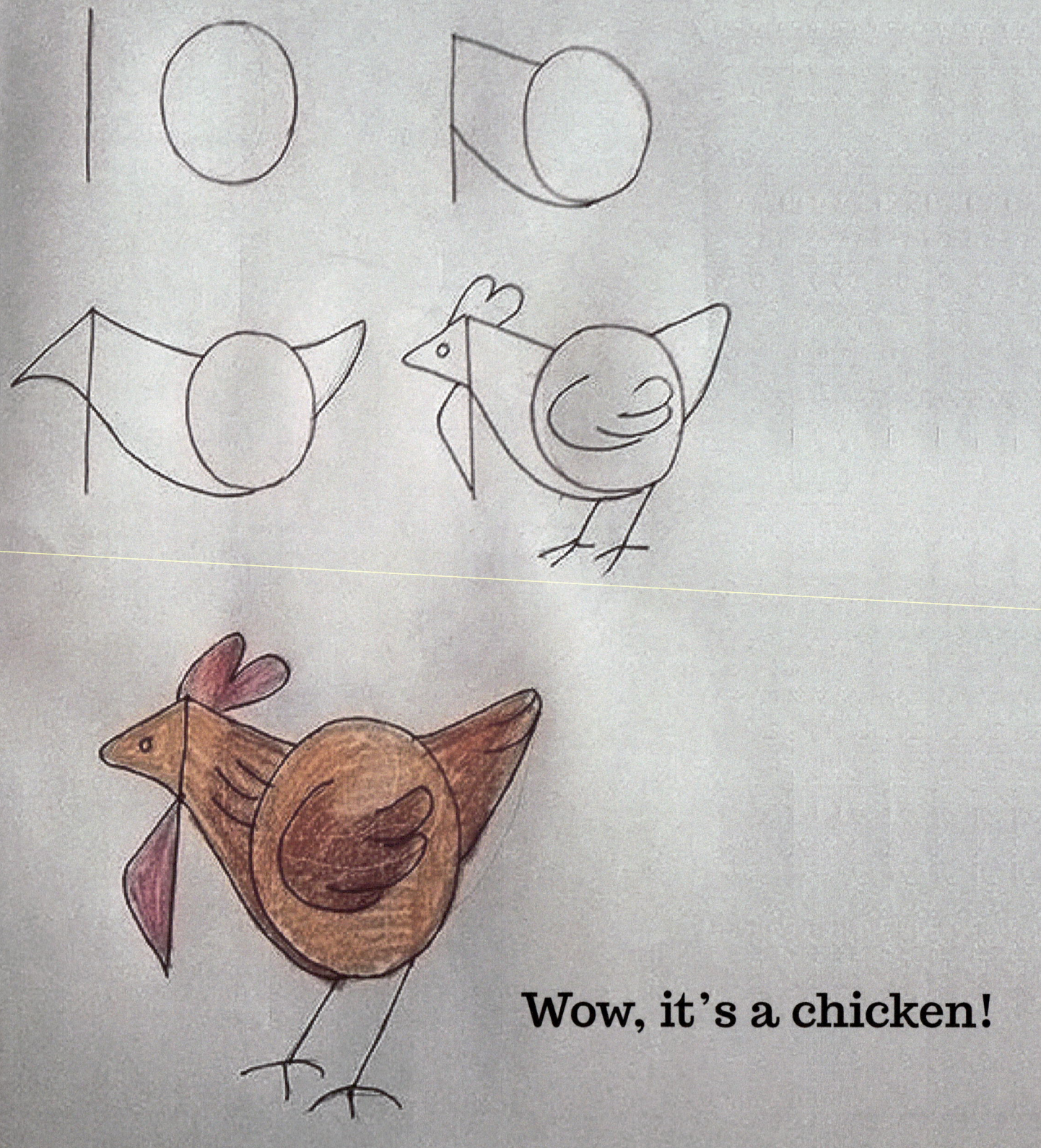

Wow, it's a chicken!

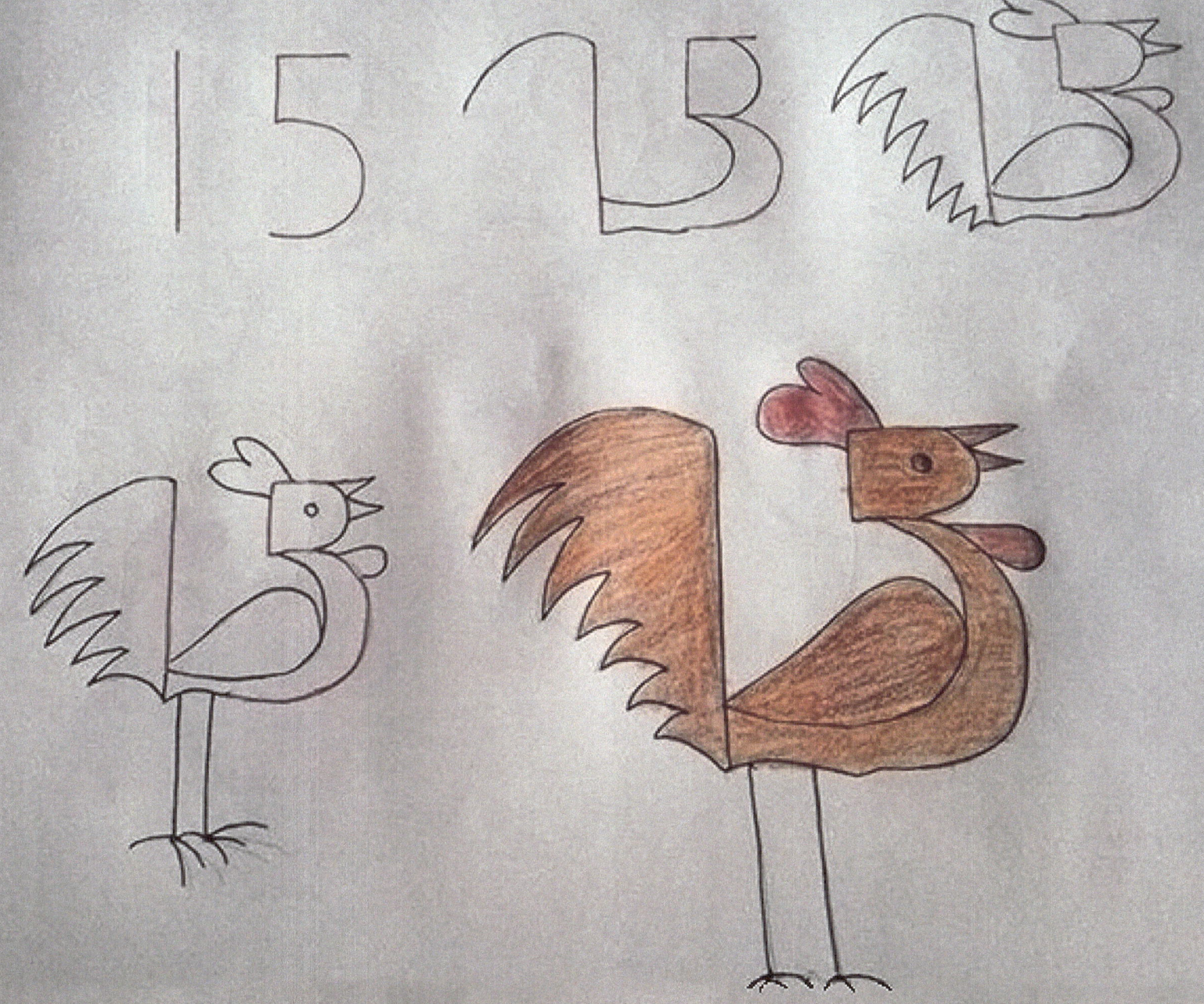

Wow, it's another chicken!

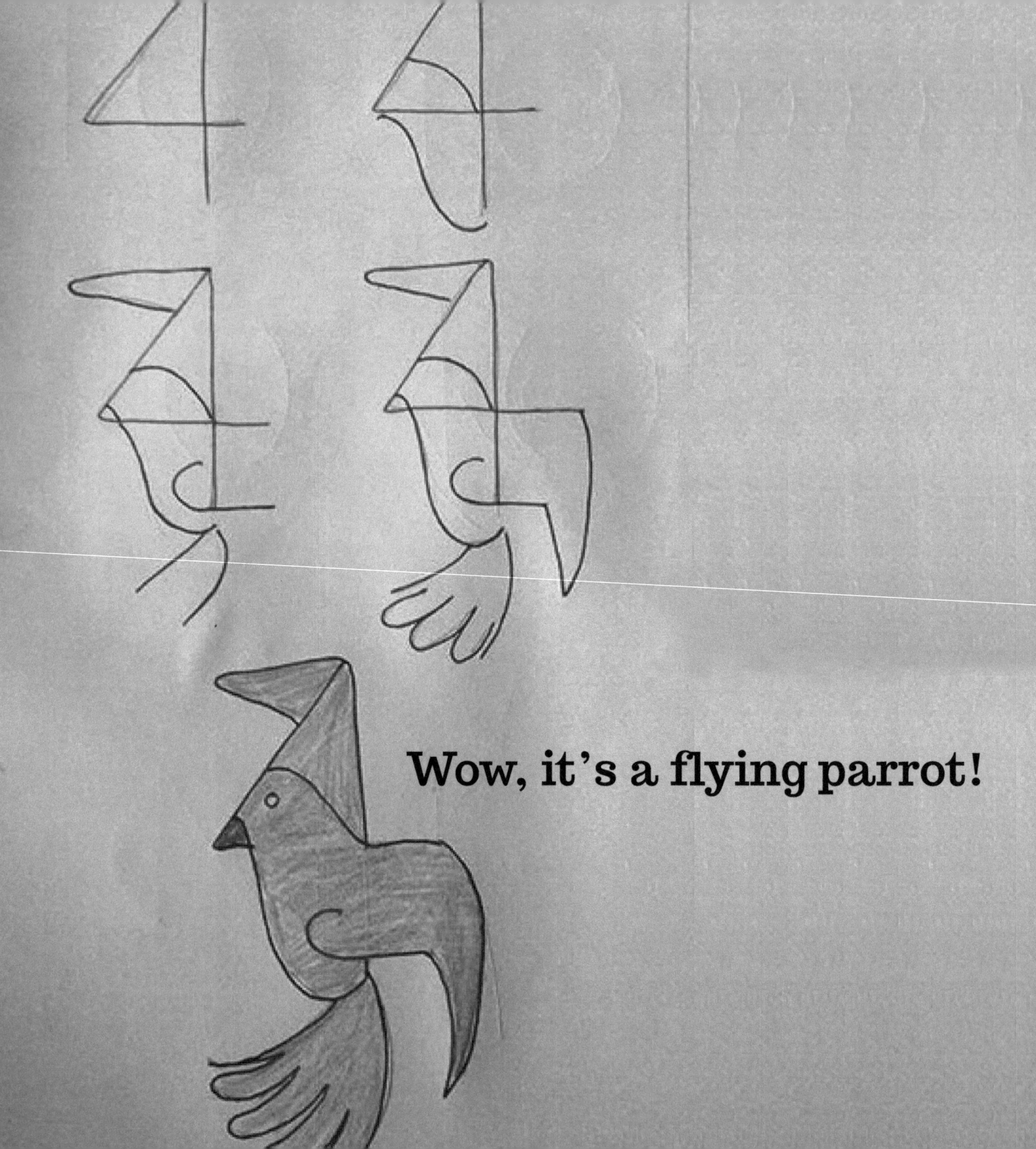

Wow, it's a flying parrot!

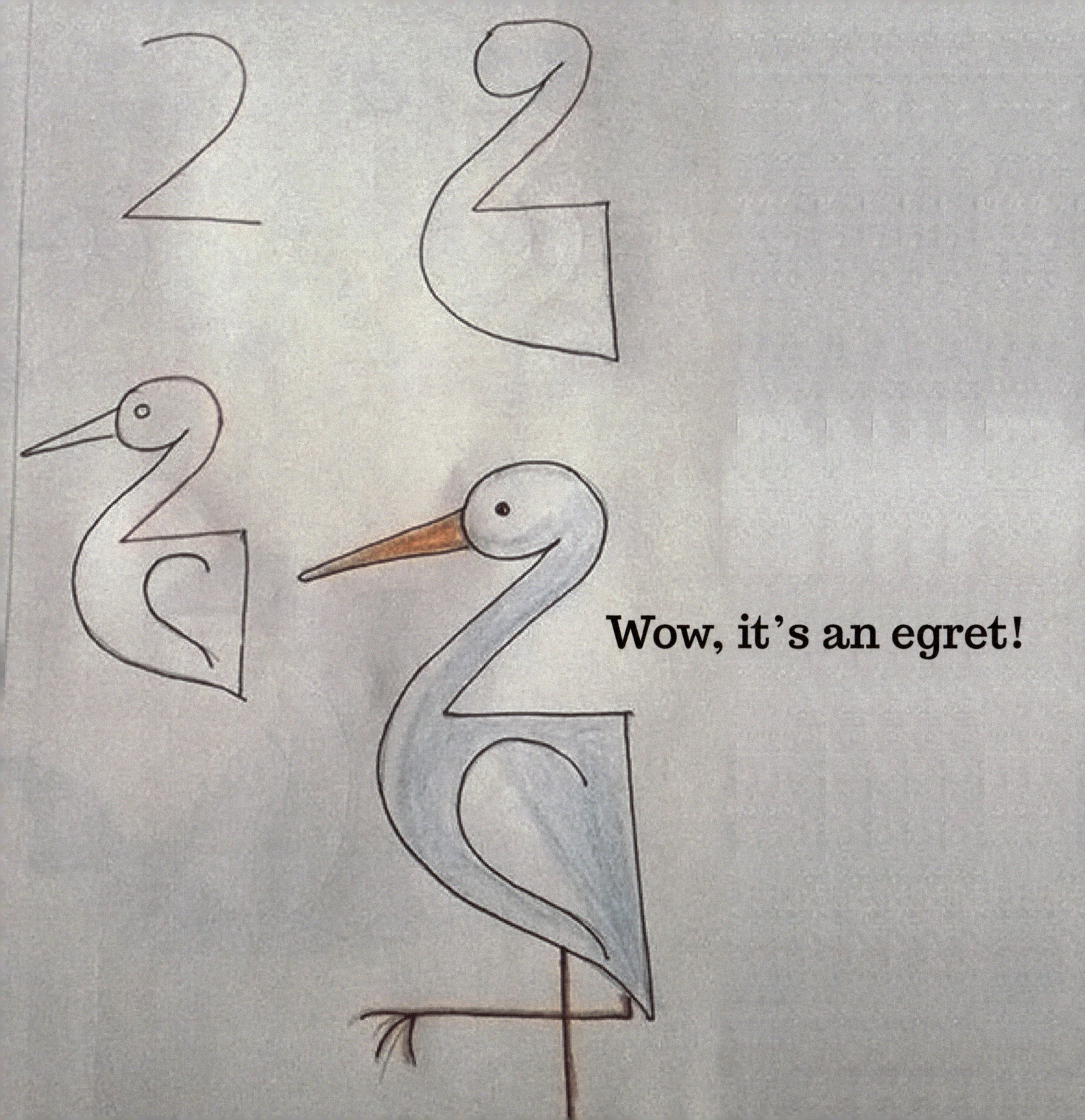

Wow, it's an egret!

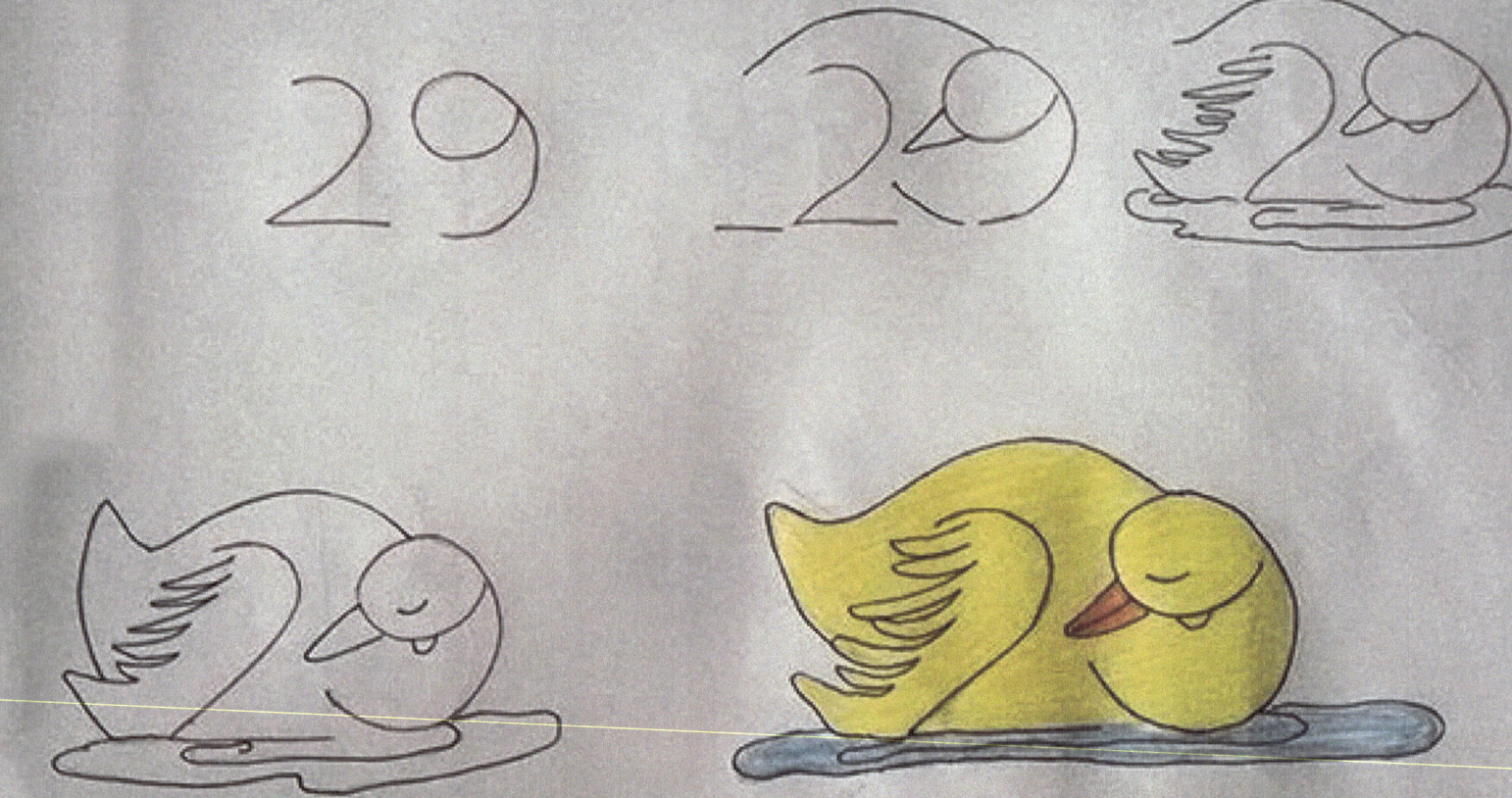

Wow, it's a duck!

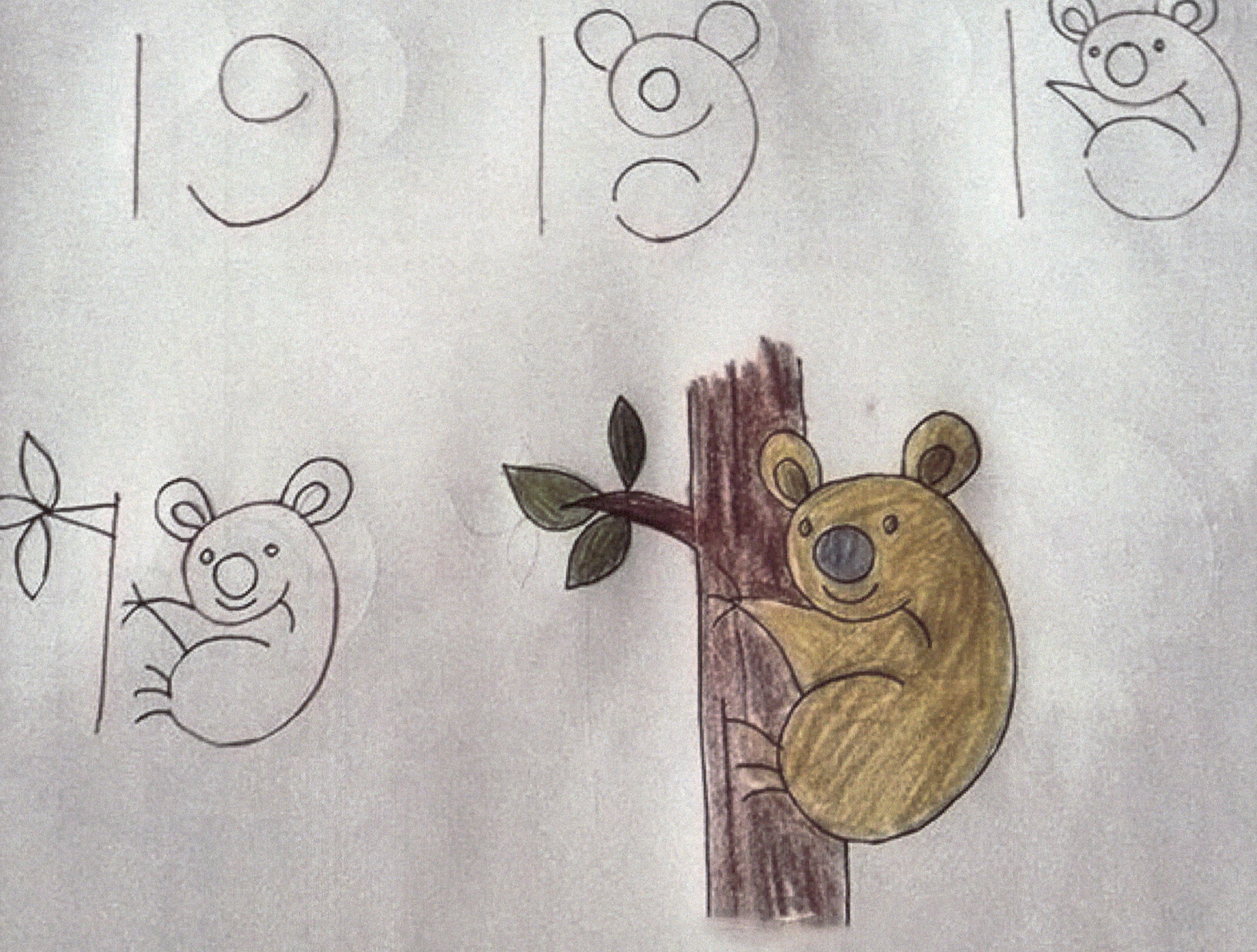

Wow, it's a little squirrel!

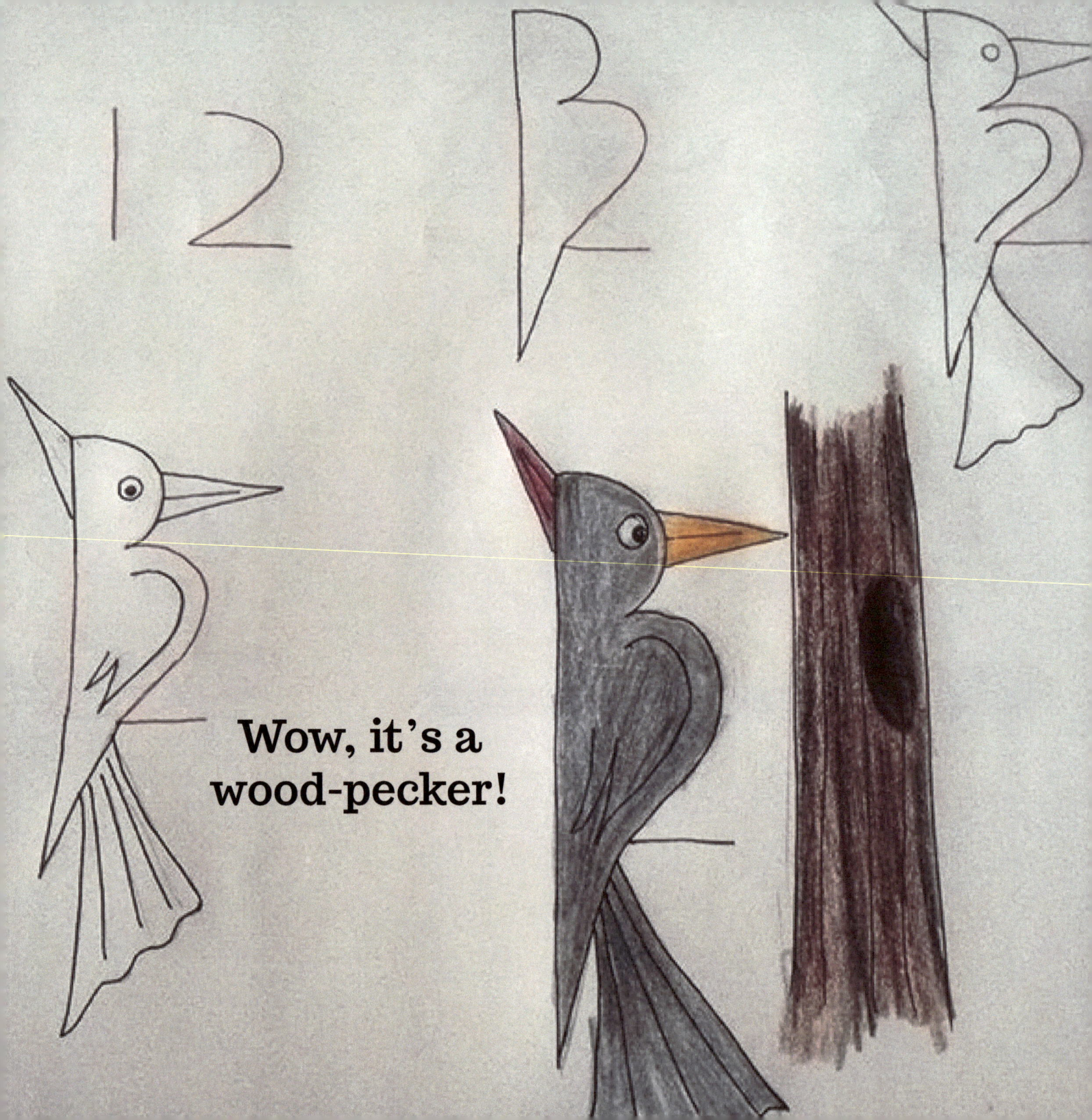

Wow, it's a wood-pecker!

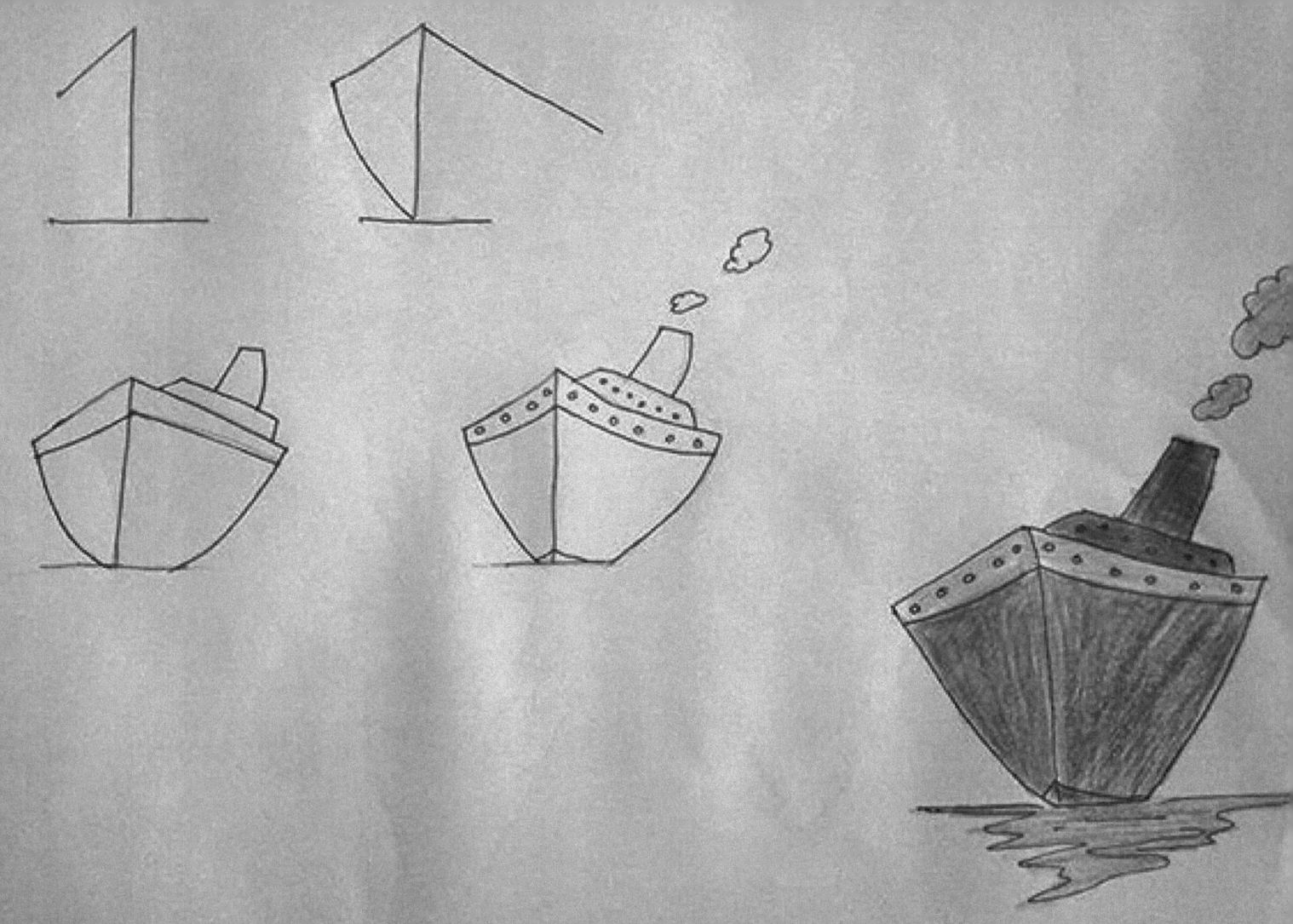

Wow, it's a ship!

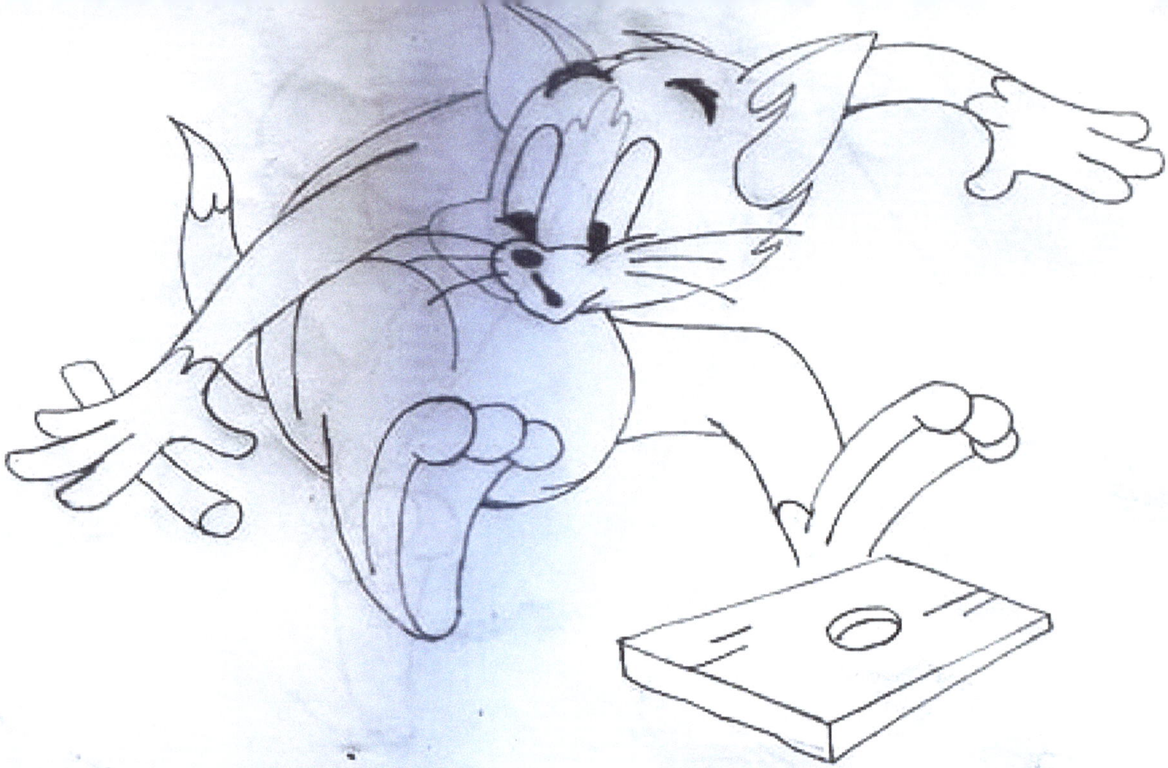

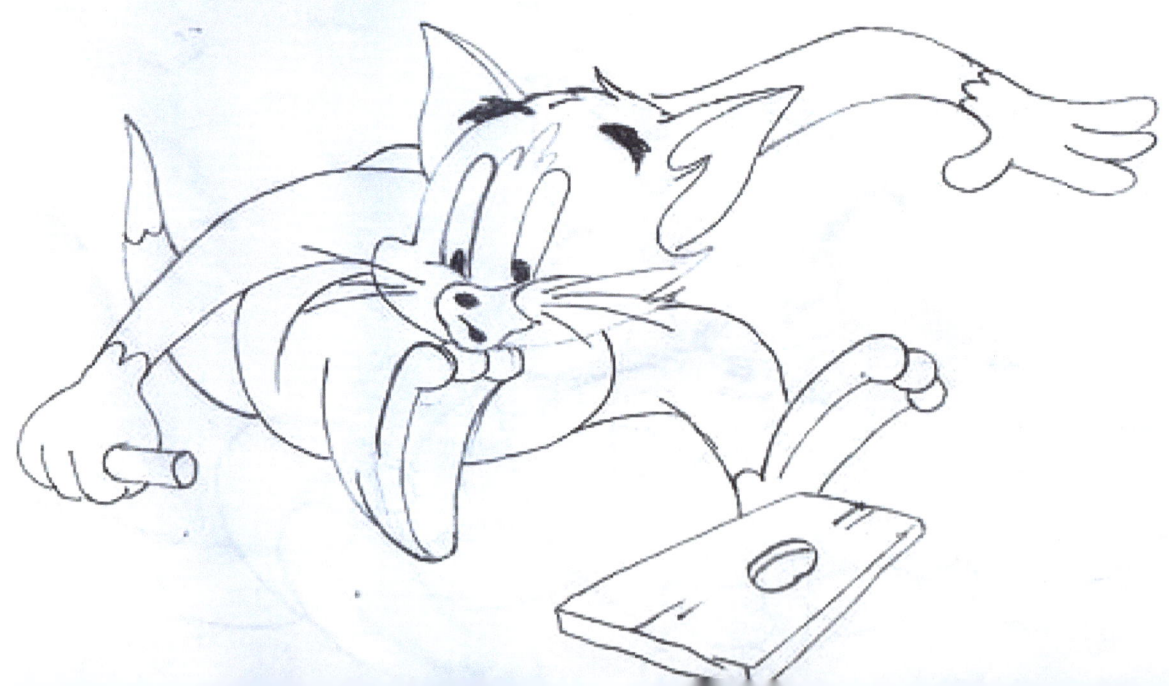

Can you color me with your pencil?

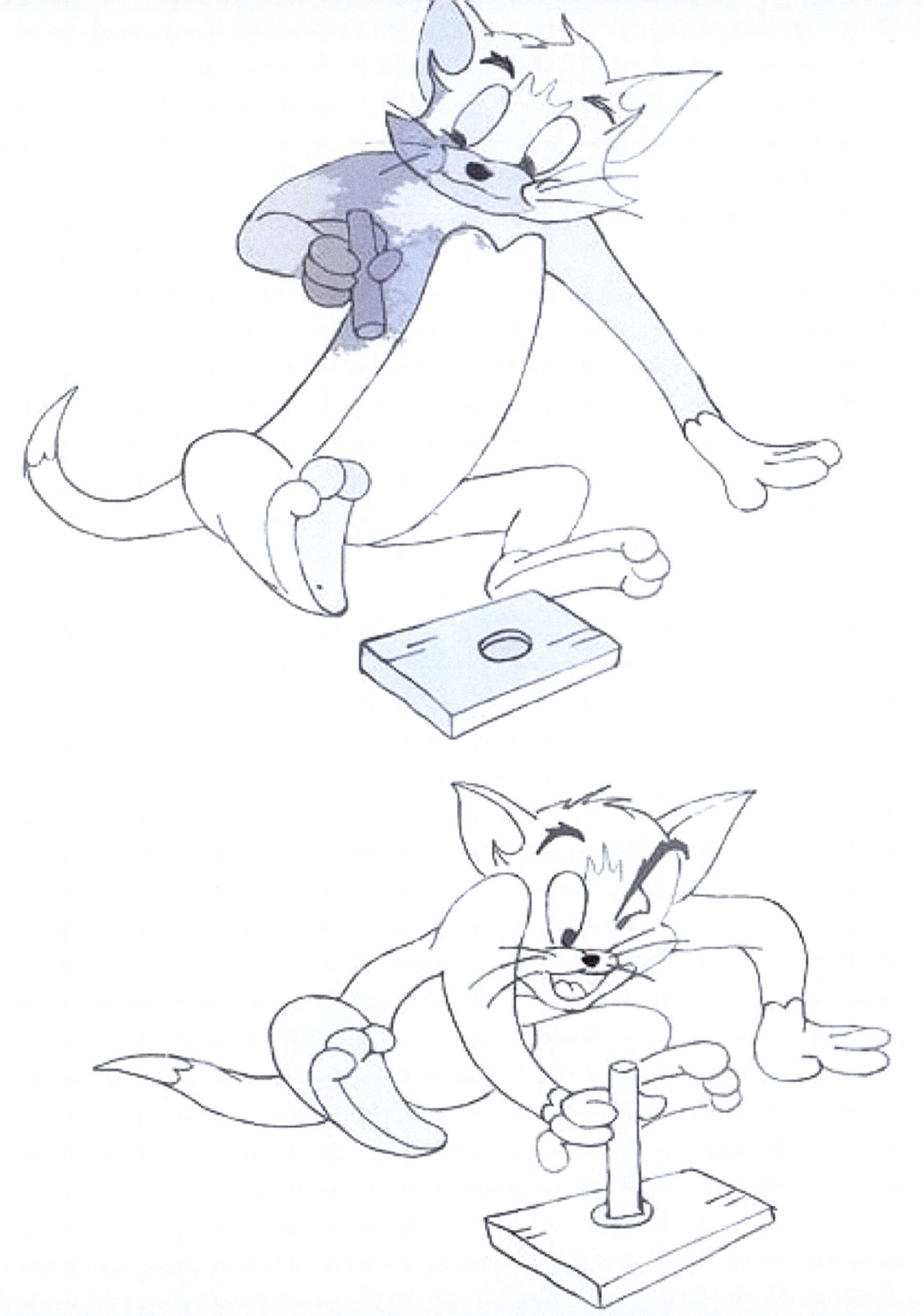

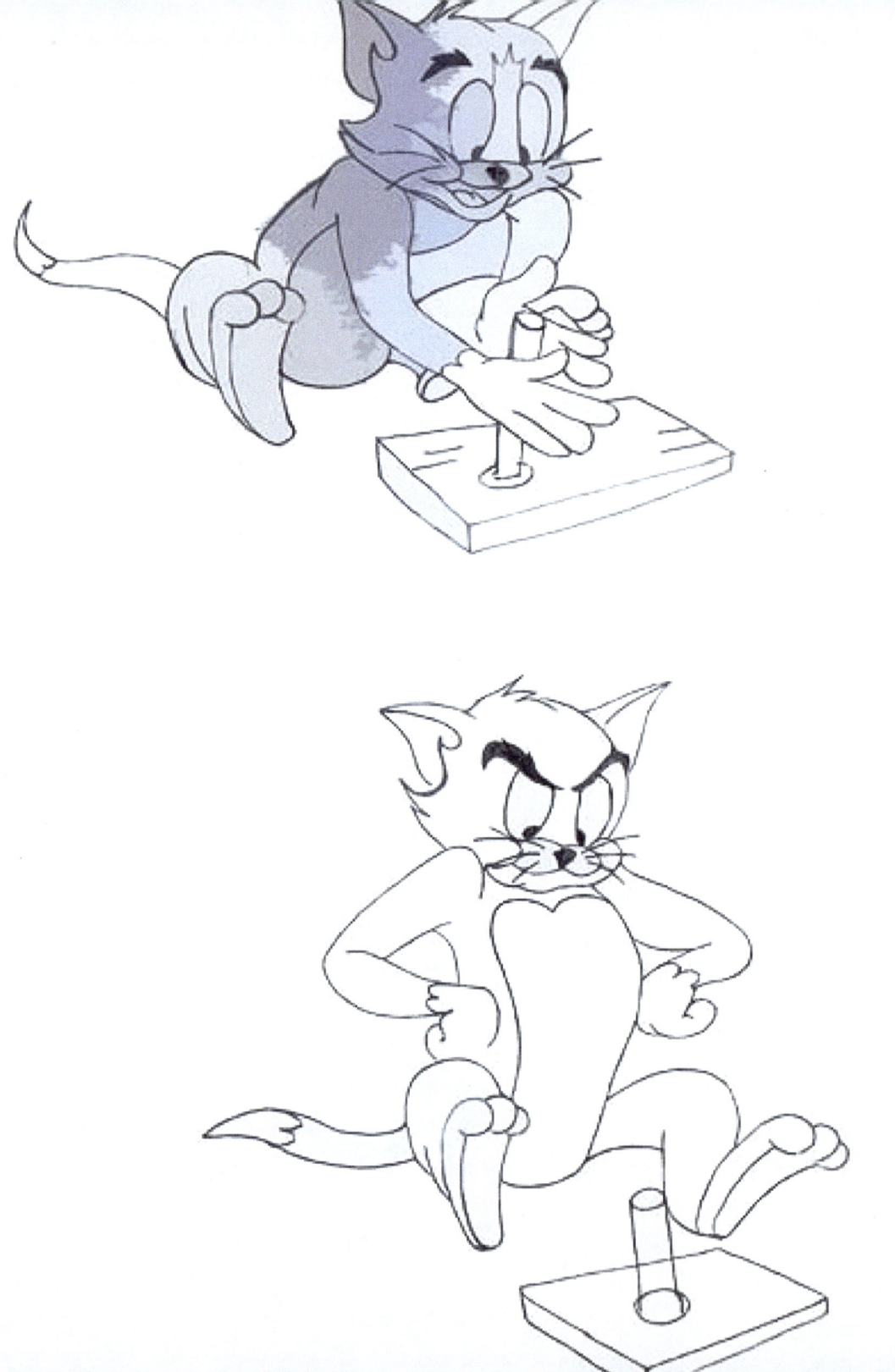

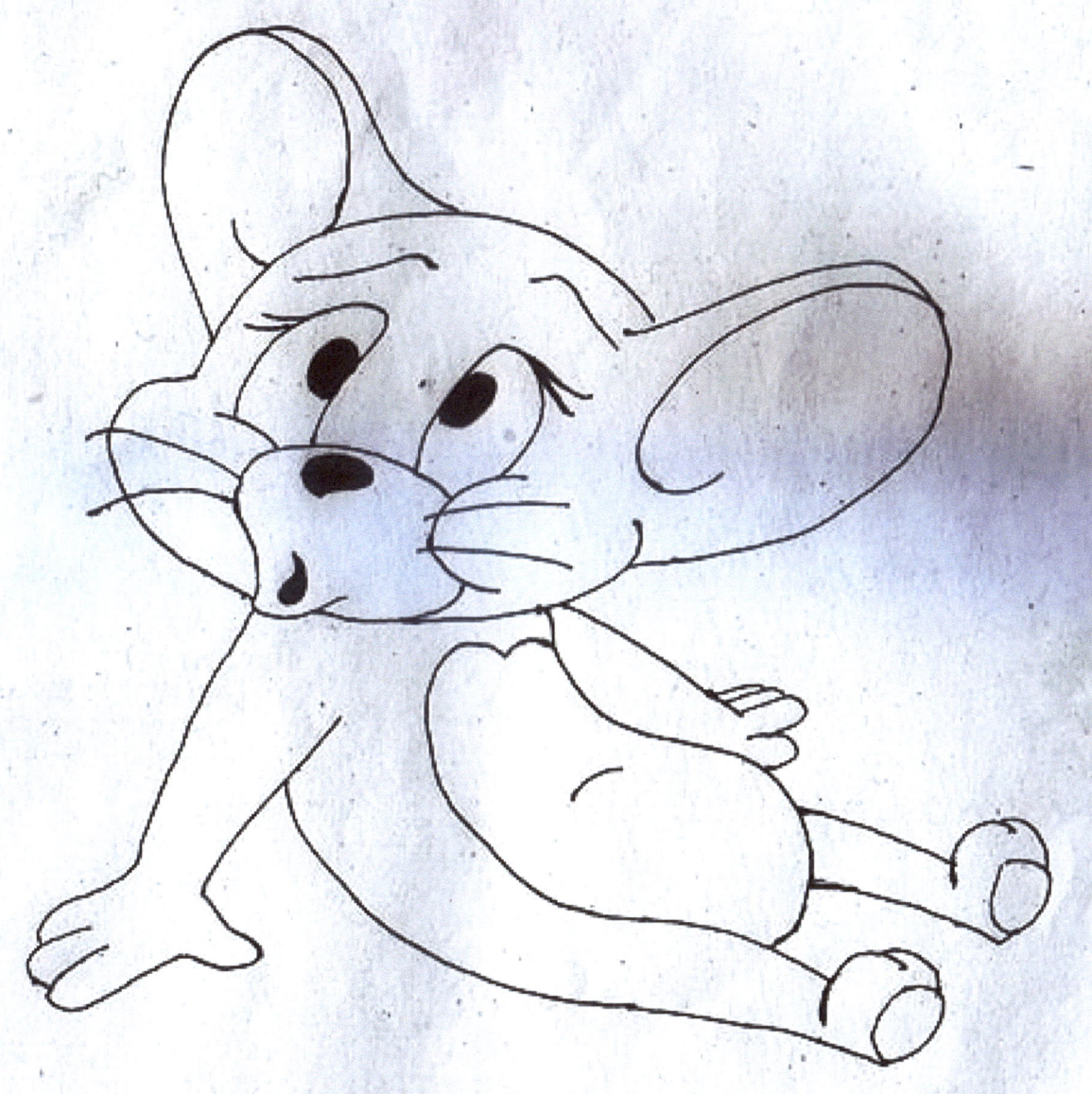

Can you color me with your pencil?

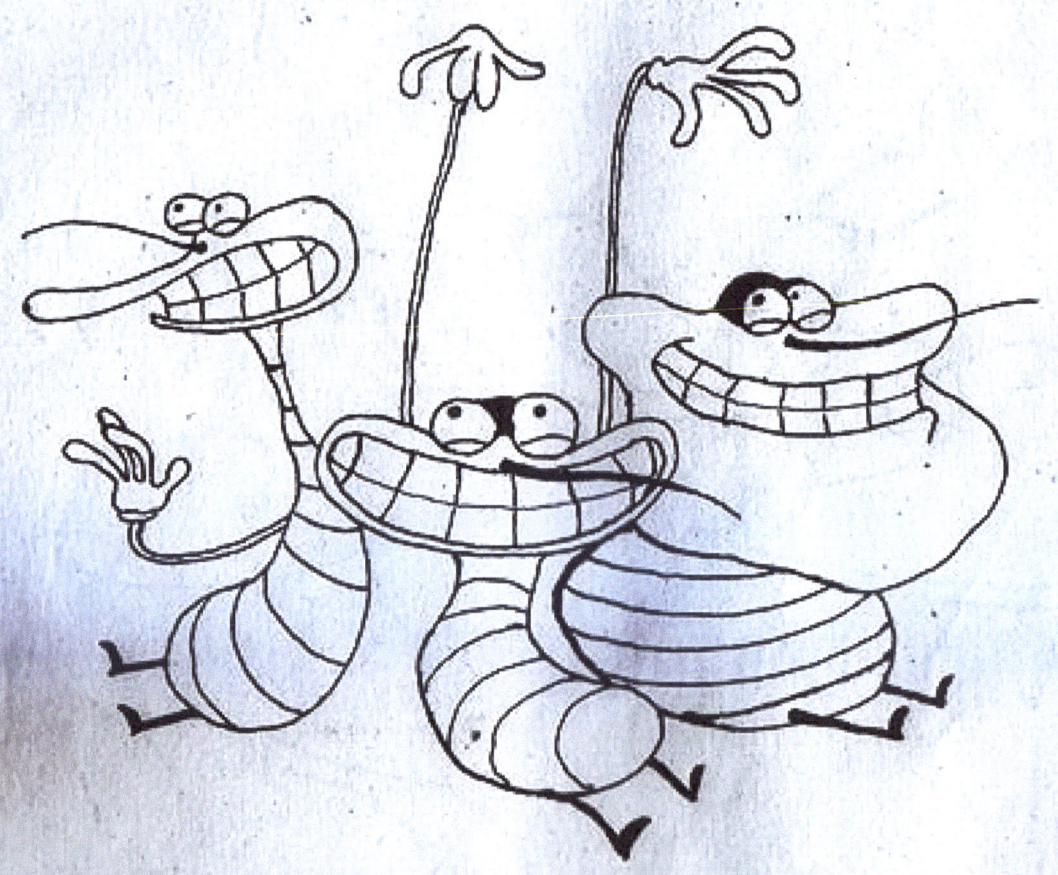

Can you color me with your pencil?

Can you color me with your pencil?

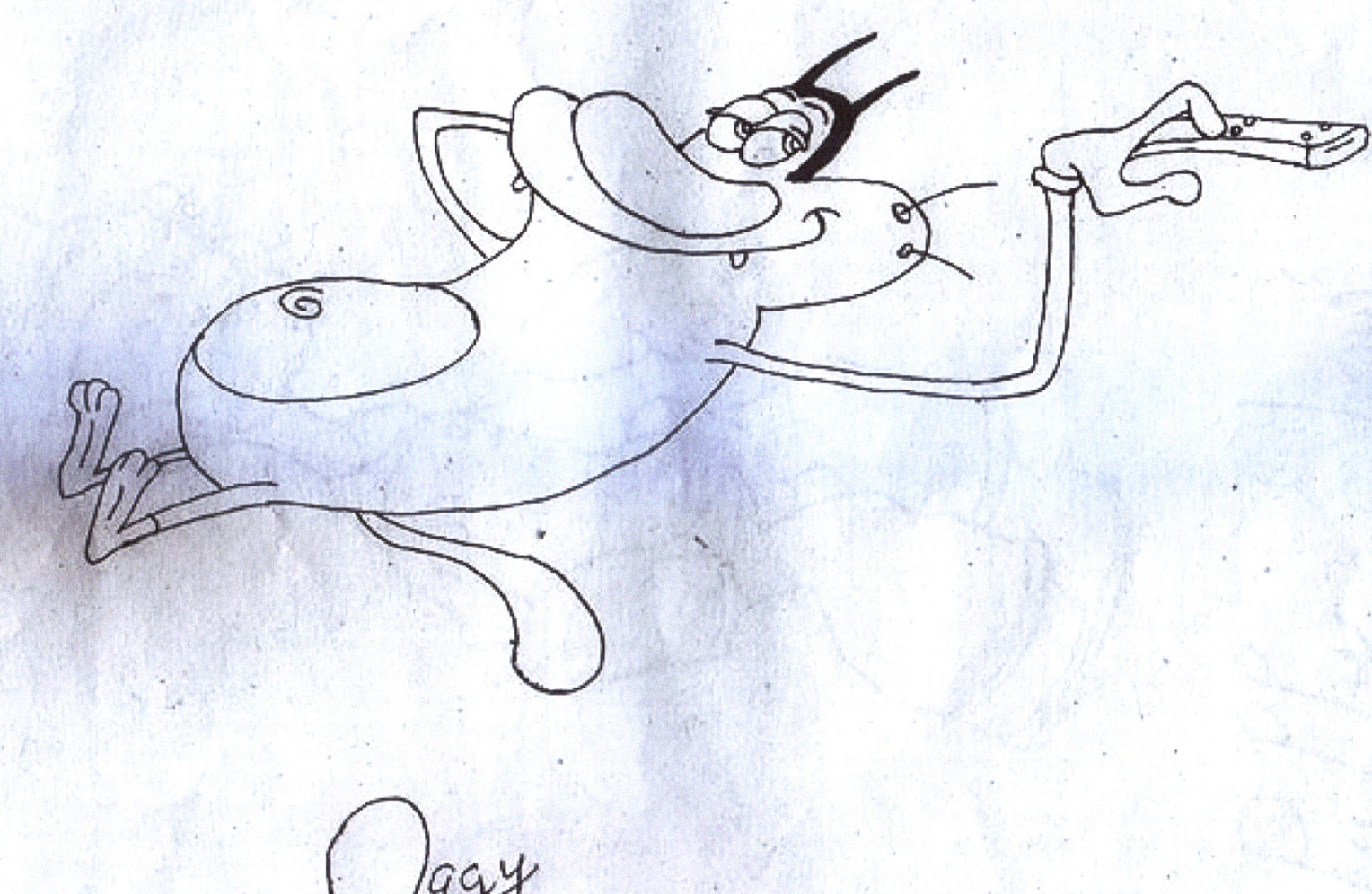

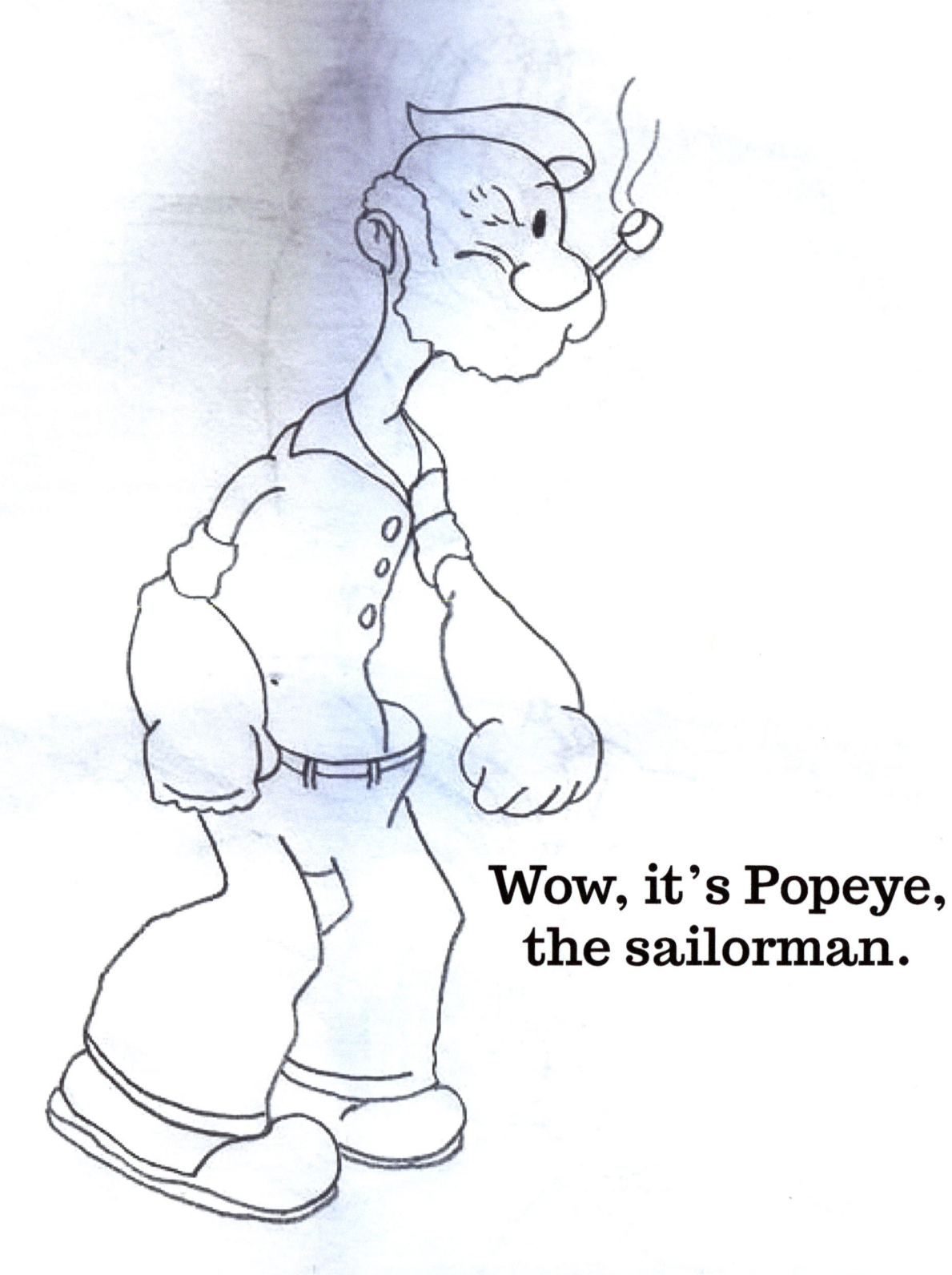

Wow, it's Popeye, the sailorman.

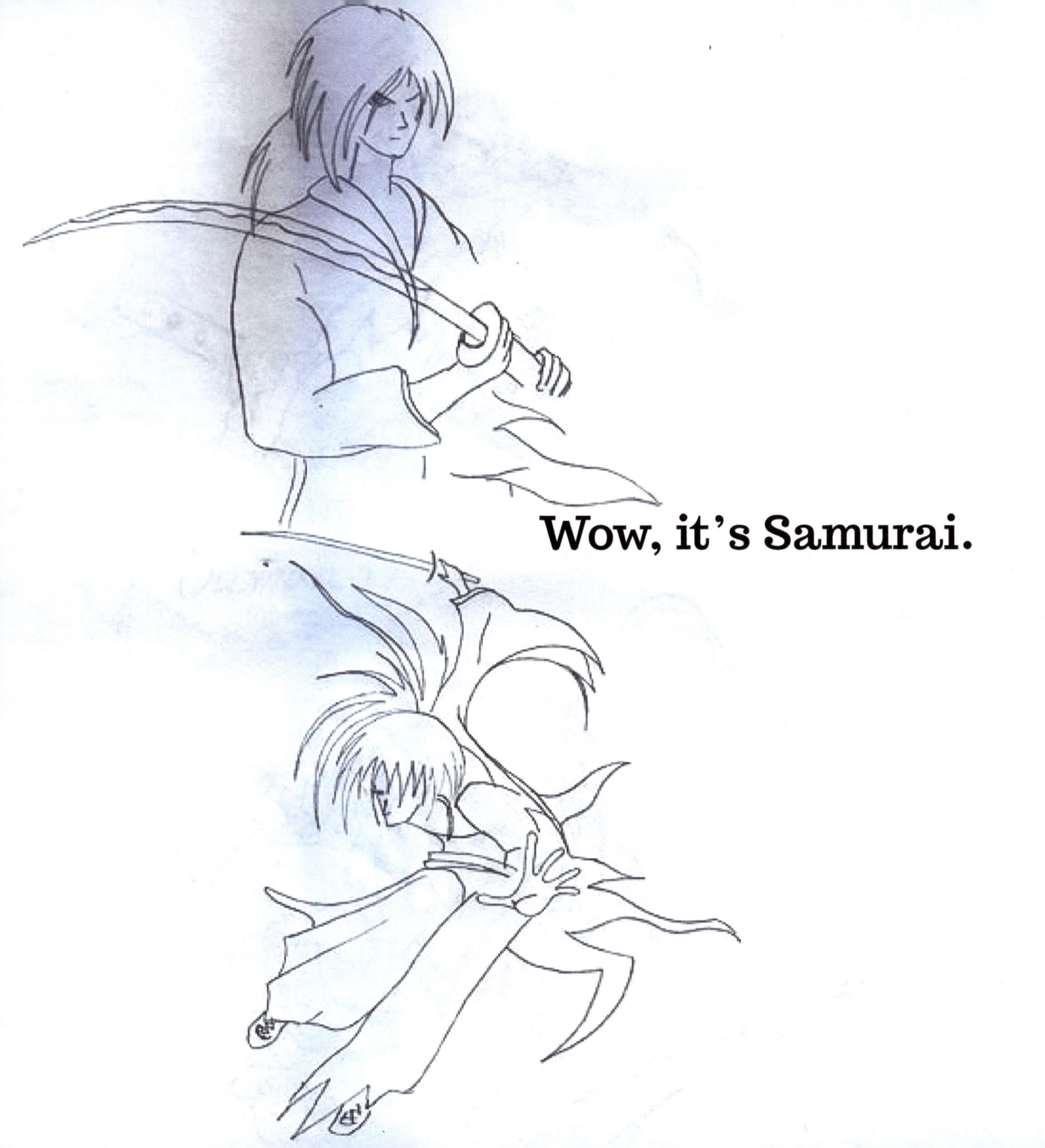

Wow, it's Samurai.

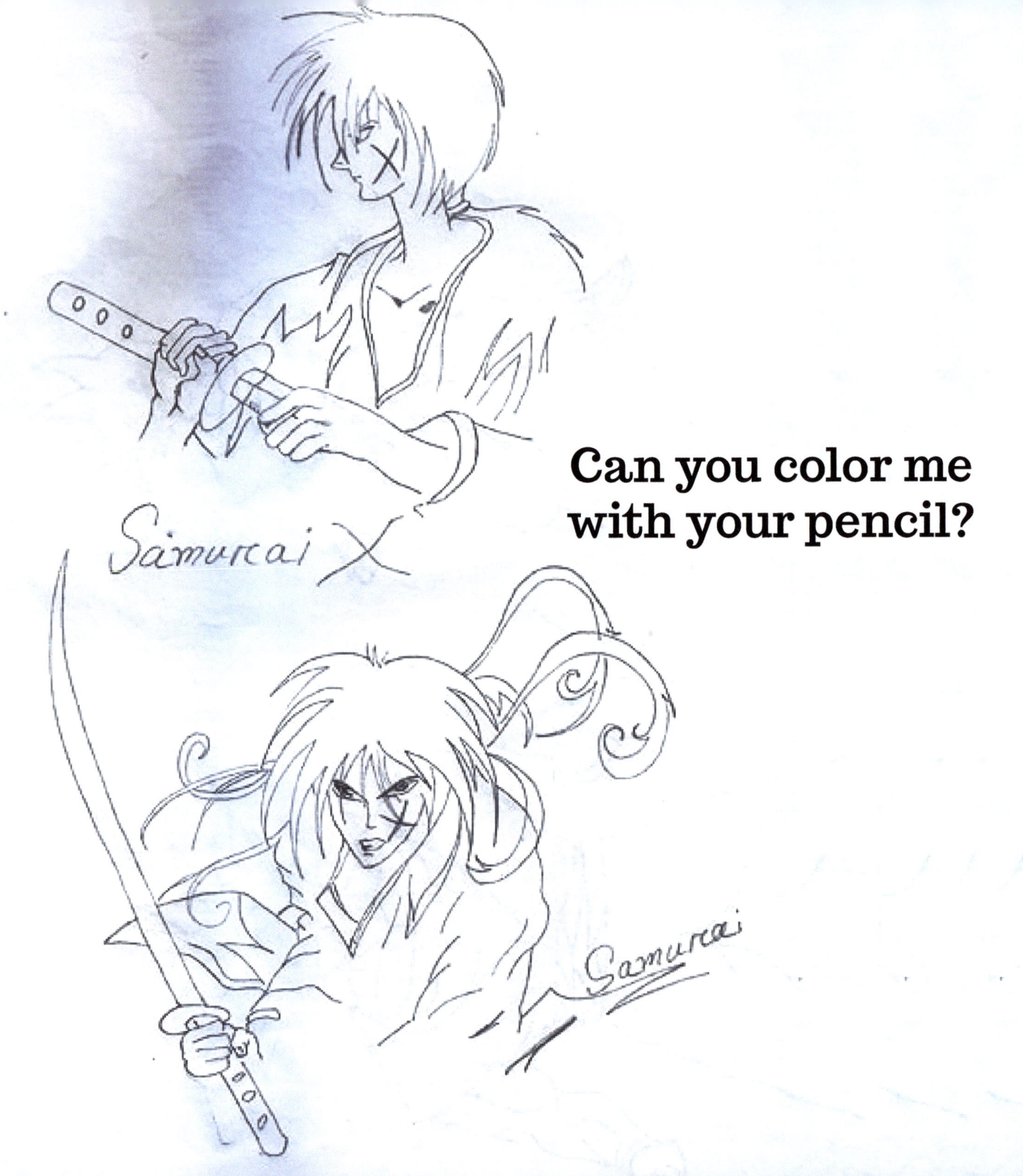

Can you color me
with your pencil?

Can you color me with your pencil?

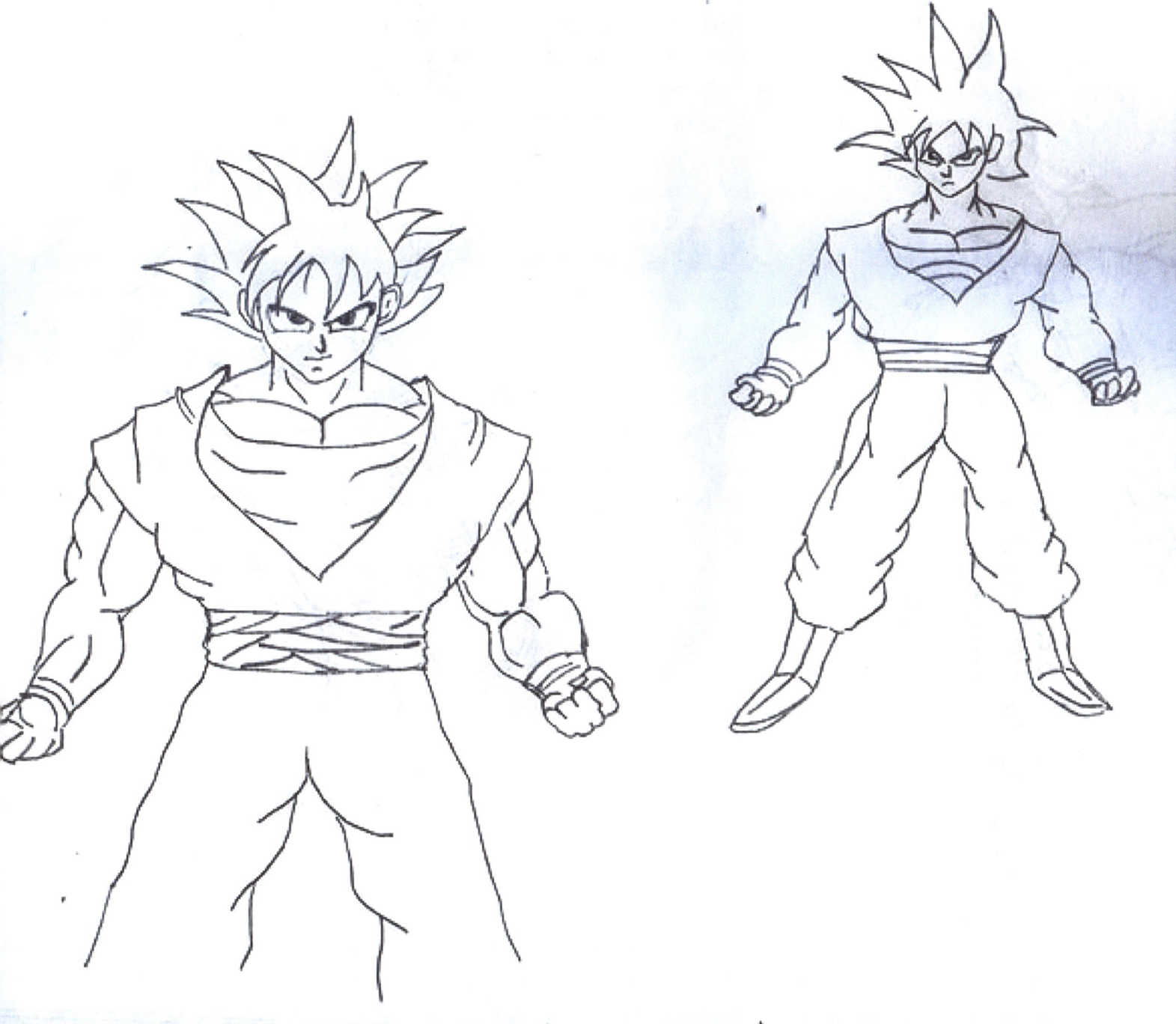

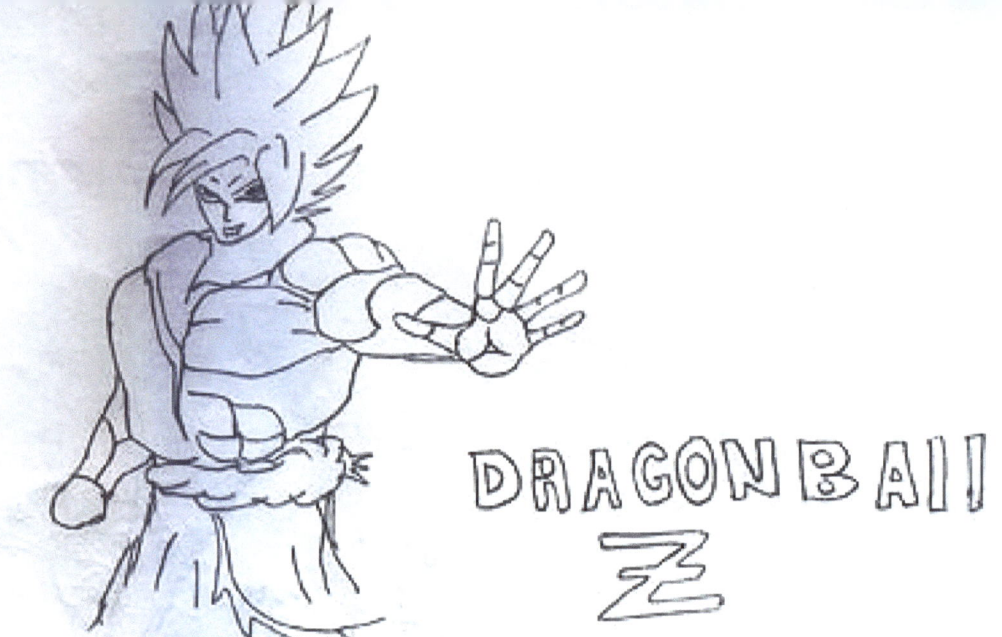

DRAGON BALL Z

Can you color us with your pencil?

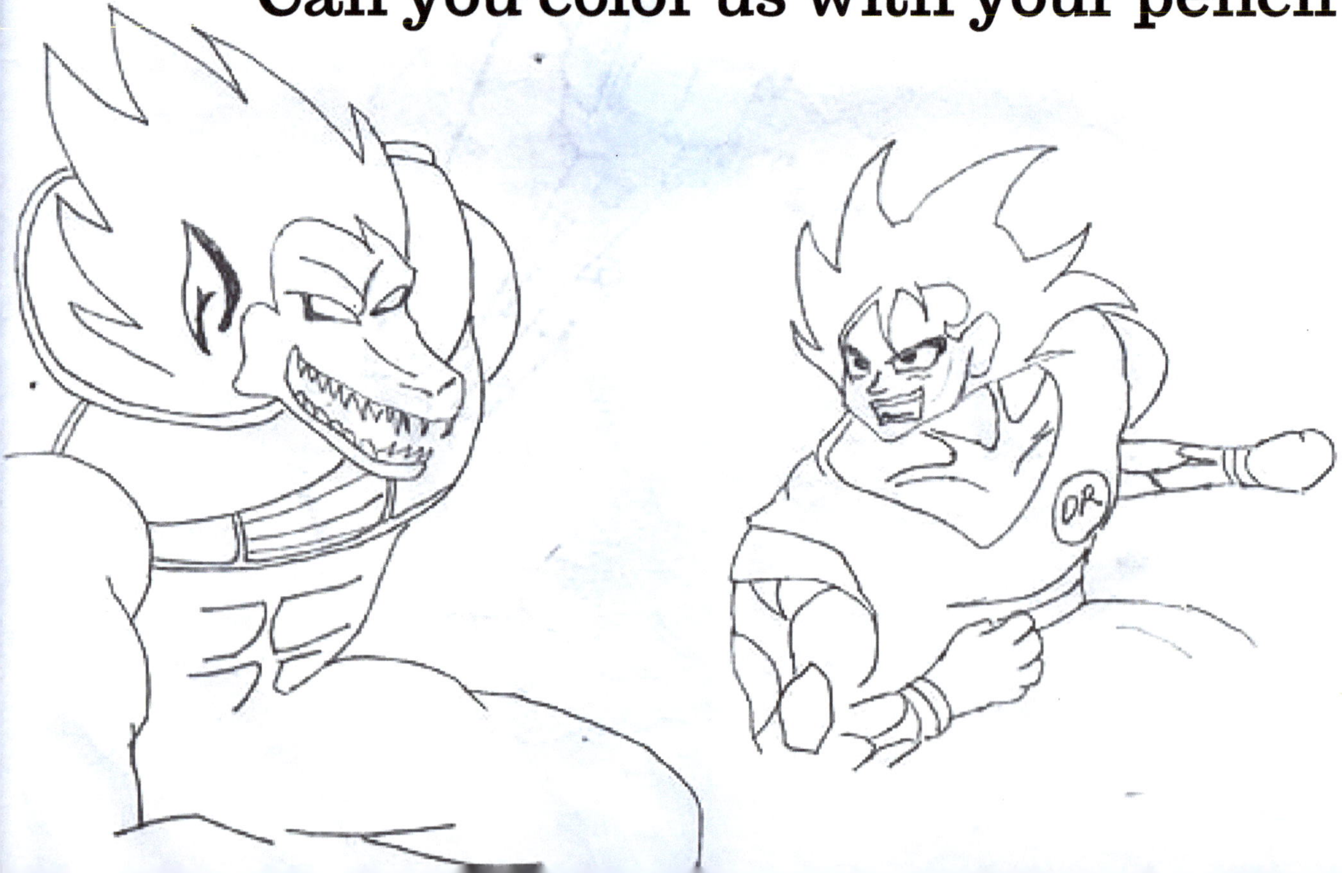

Can you color me with your pencil?

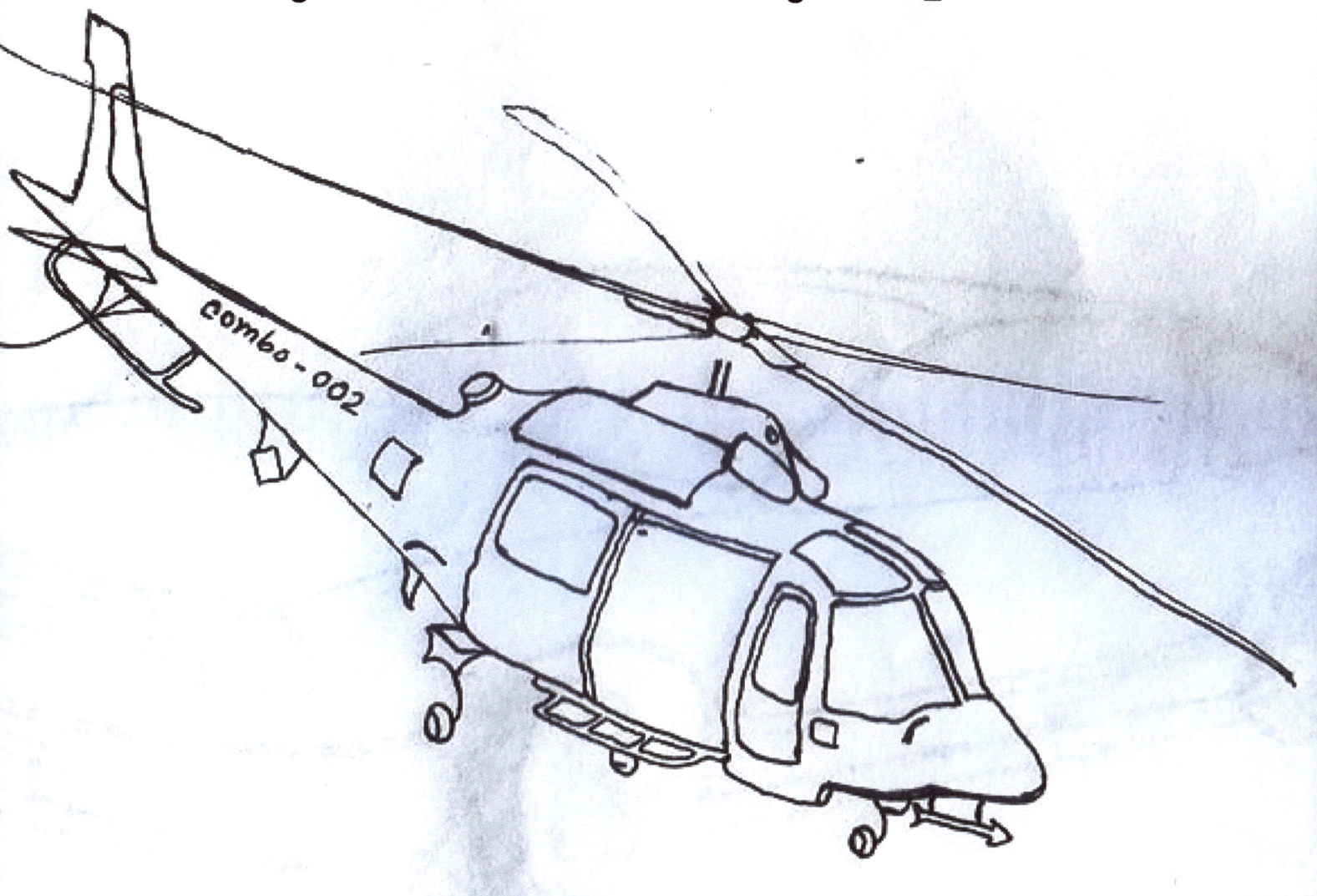

Can you color me with your pencil?

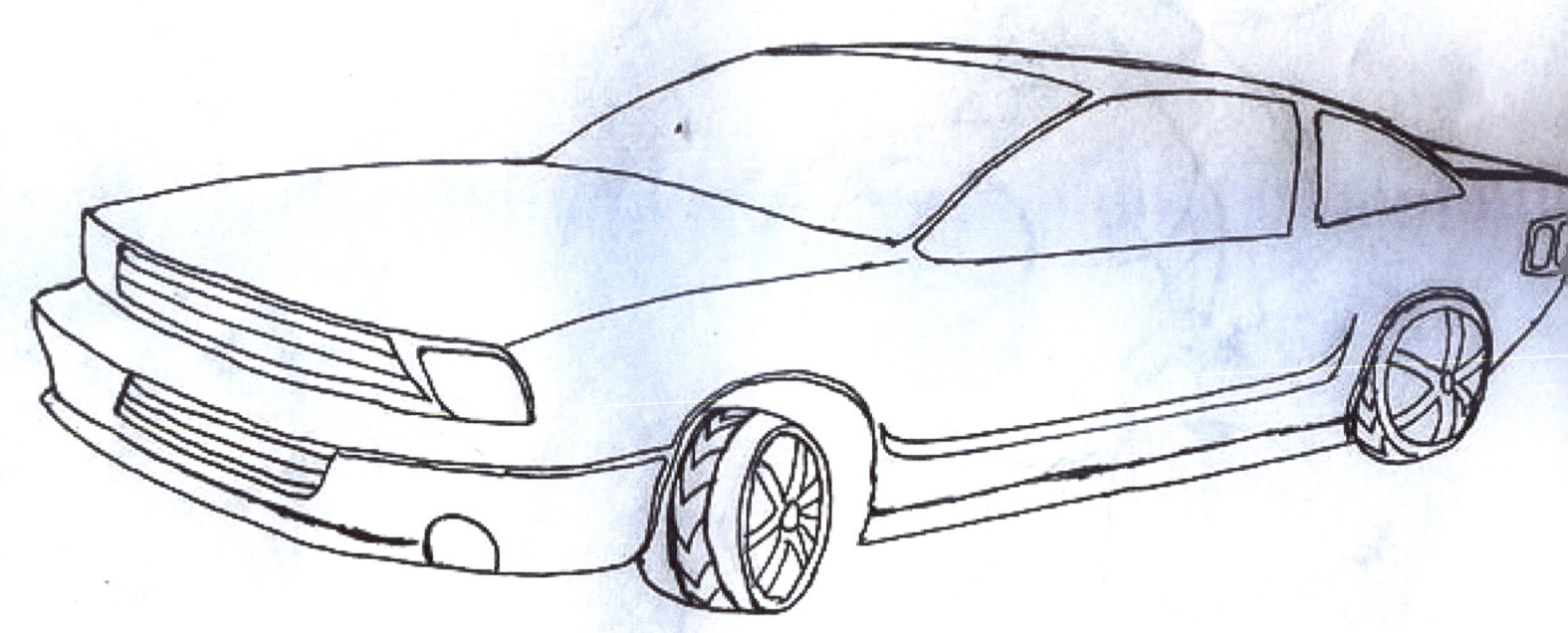

Yahoo, we are already colored!

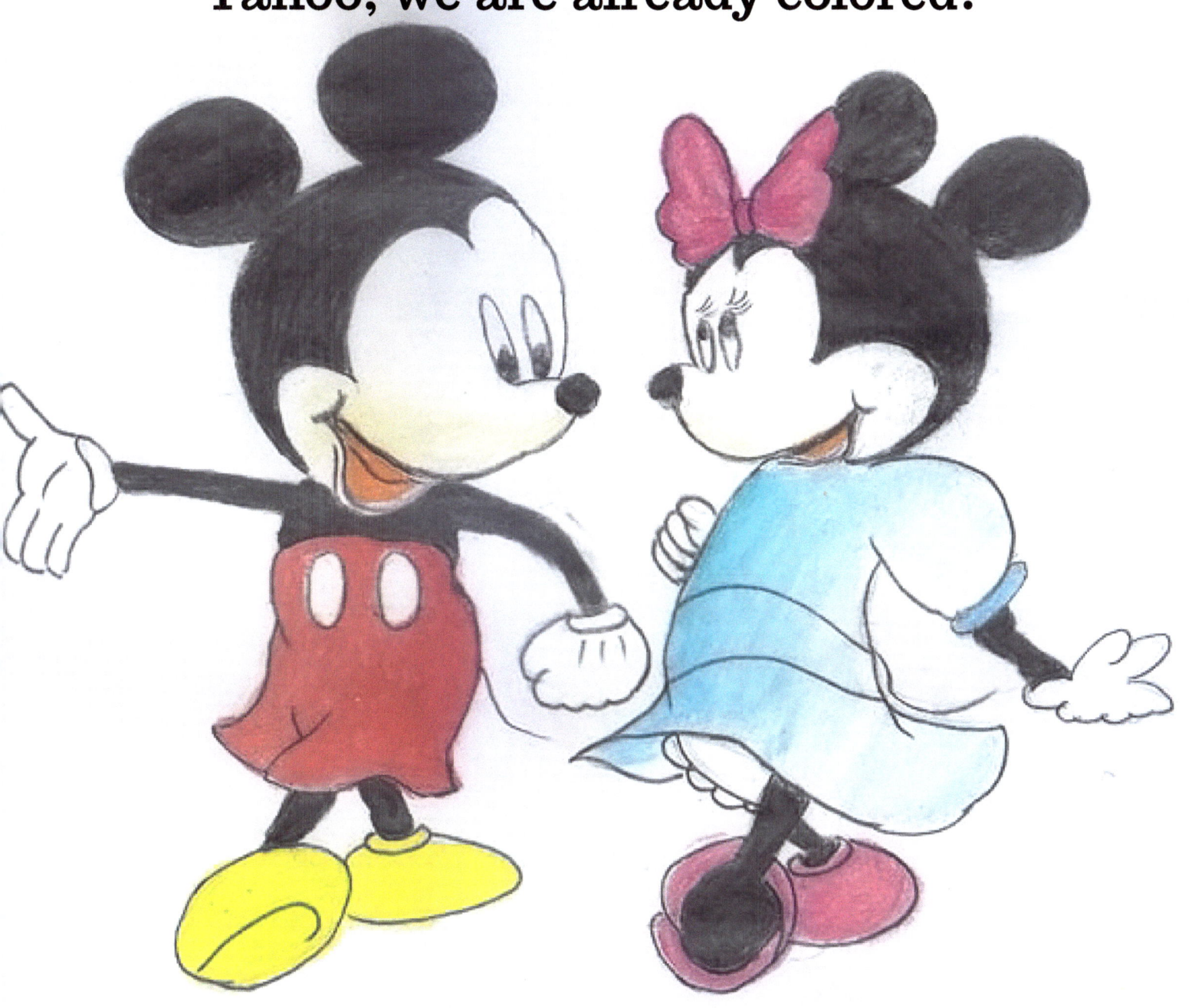

Did you like us?

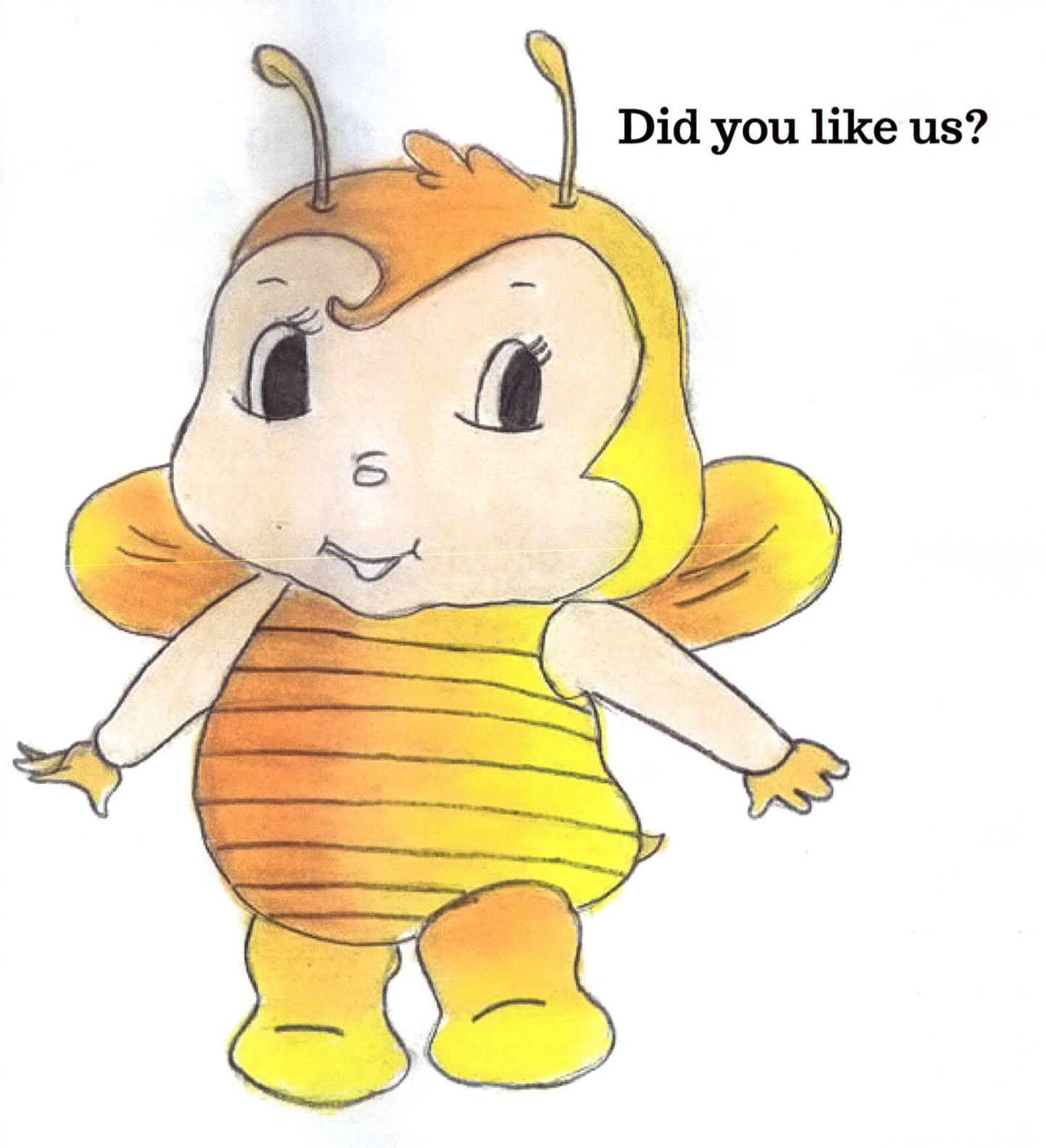

Please leave a positive
review for us.

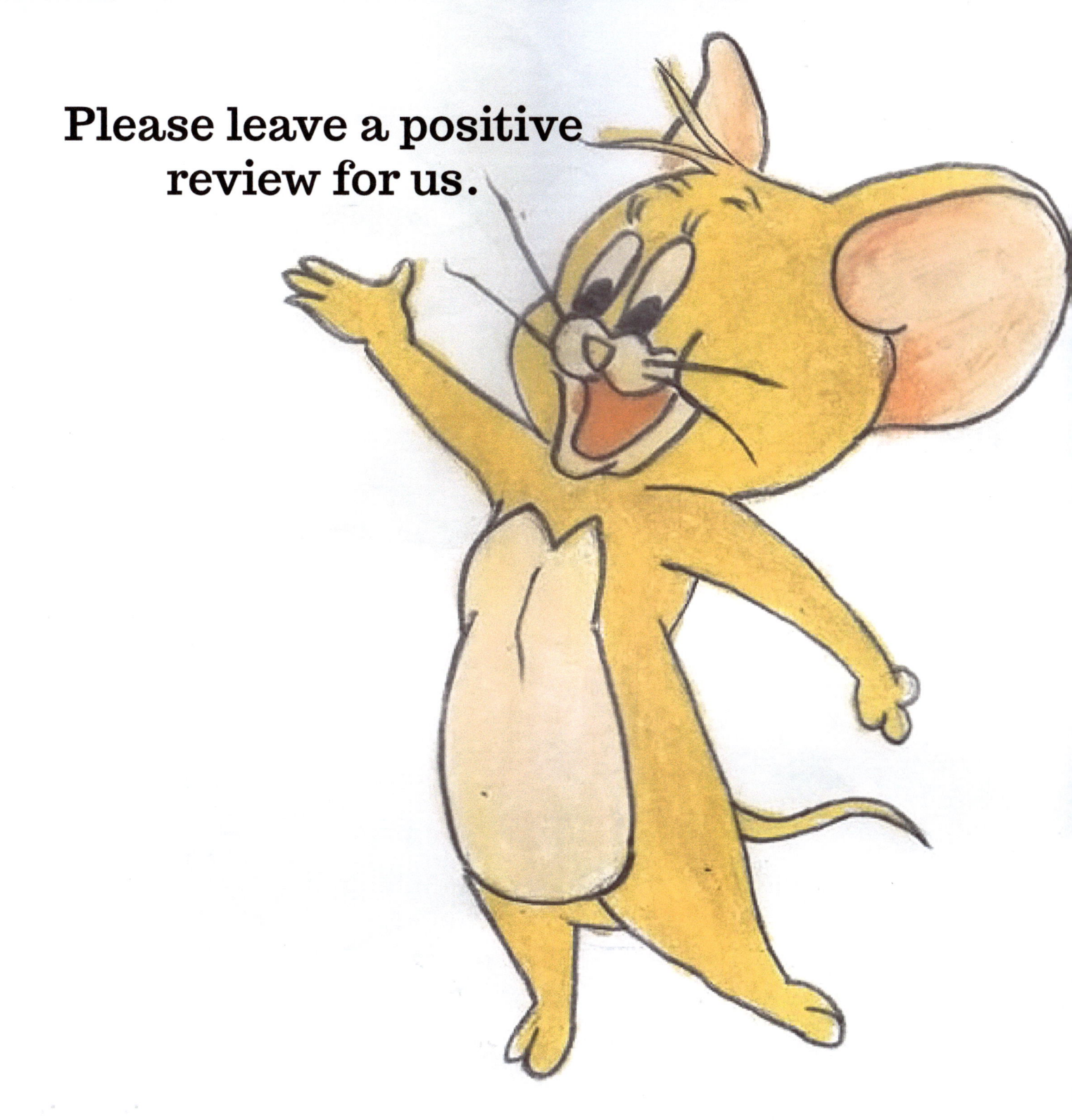